Like a Butterfly, I've Come alive

Anita Dwyer

authorHOUSE®

AuthorHouse™
1663 Liberty Drive
Bloomington, IN 47403
www.authorhouse.com
Phone: 1 (800) 839-8640

Published by AuthorHouse 06/24/2015

ISBN: 978-1-5049-1915-9 (sc)
ISBN: 978-1-5049-1914-2 (e)

Print information available on the last page.

Any people depicted in stock imagery provided by Thinkstock are models,
and such images are being used for illustrative purposes only.
Certain stock imagery © Thinkstock.

This book is printed on acid-free paper.

Because of the dynamic nature of the Internet, any web addresses or links contained in
this book may have changed since publication and may no longer be valid. The views
expressed in this work are solely those of the author and do not necessarily reflect the
views of the publisher, and the publisher hereby disclaims any responsibility for them.

I wish to dedicate this book to my two children,

my son, Bill and Victoria

my daughter, Donna and George

and to thank them for what they have become.

I'm so proud of you all and the choices you

have made.

And to Carl, who has brought me out of my

"cacoon" and has shown me how to enjoy our

senior years together. It is true, laughter is the

best medicine.

Love,

Mom, M.I.L. Anita

June 2015

What does a "nobody" have to write about? Her life? Her love? Well, you may be surprised what a history an 88 year old can collect over the years. Some of my history may surprise you and you are never too old to learn. Oh yeah, thanks to Bill Clinton and a few others, I may shock you, so read on.

As far as being "someone" you may have read about, forget it. I'm not a celebrity or politician. If I were either, you would have heard, as it seems, both have a habit of breaking rules, going to jail or committing suicide. My life is too precious to do anything but live it to the fullest. Oh you want to know what makes me think you will read this, well, aren't you reading it to find out what makes me feel I have something to write about? So, sit back, get that box of bon bons, put your feet up and enjoy.

My life started in Beverly, Massachusetts in 1926, wow that's a long time ago, wouldn't you agree? Anywho, I was the youngest of 5 children born to legal Americans, my mother came from Russia and my father from Italy. I like to say I have roman hands and rushing fingers. ha ha. A bit of wit.

I had 3 sisters, Helen, Rita and Gloria and a brother Maxwell. I was the youngest. I want to thank my grammar school kids for chasing me home, calling me a WOP because of my Italian name, Perrotta. I truly believe this gave me a new strength, thank you.

As I was a left handed student, when I was in third grade, Mrs. Stephens, (funny how you never forget a name that made a change in your life), kept me after school and taught me to write right handed. To this day, I do everything else left handed but, because of the changing of writing, I can write with both hands at the same time, right hand is correct and left hand is mirror image. I'm working on becoming somebody.

Growing up during the "Great Depression", I'll never know why they called it "Great," but I look back to those years and think of it as giving me strength and a strong will to survive. My Pop worked, and I mean worked for the WPA, a government way of giving a little to help during the "Great Depression". It was NOT like the Welfare of today, you worked, did not hold your hand out for doing nothing.. A penny was a lot of money to me. When my friend Dearie and I had a penny, we would go to Keenan's and push our noses on the candy display glass and spend a good time deciding what we could share.

Also, at the age of 6 or 7, I went around the neighborhood with my red wagon selling cucumbers from our garden, three for ten cents. Why do I tell you this? Well, I knew something about showmanship. I nailed my building blocks to the heels of my shoes and I pretended they were "high heels". I sold a lot of cukes. Cute, huh?

Won't you buy my cukes?

Being the youngest, I didn't get the chance to make mistakes. My siblings did the mistakes and I learned from them. I think I was spoiled, got to go with my sisters even when they didn't want me. All I had to do was cry to Mama and they were stuck with me.

For instance, 2 of my sisters got pregnant before marriage, heaven forbid. So I learned from my mother not to let that happen to me. At age 15 or there about, she told me to ensure I didn't get pregnant, put an aspirin between my knees. Do you know how hard that is to do? To walk? True fact, when I married at age 21, I was a virgin, not be to confused with Viagra and the aspirin had nothing to do with it.

I had my first job at age 16, at the local variety store owned by the Keenan's. I loved it! Along with dry goods, there was a lending library and I believe that is where I got my love of books.

1942, WW2 was being fought and as Mrs. Keenan was a true supporter of the war and the servicemen, she put a large map of the world in the front window and with ribbons, marking locations as to where our local men were stationed. There was Nemo, Vince, Hughie, to name a few, and as I was 16 and in love with all the guys, I would write them letters, they were so long, I'd scroll them up, put an airmail stamp on them and off they would go across the world.

Do you remember your first kiss? I still do. Norma's dad had an old Ford Model T in the front yard and on September 14, 1942, Norma, Arlene, Leo and I were talking when Norma said it was my 16th birthday and I'd never been kissed by a boy. With a little encouragement, Leo chased my round and round the old car. When "I let him" catch me, he kissed me and "wow" as I sank to the running board of the car I thought what I have been missing. uumm I still think of it.

As my sisters all played a musical instrument, piano, violin and harmonica, I decided I wanted to play something. Well the violin appealed to me so I went to the music store, picked out a violin and bow BUT, as I am left handed, they restrung the strings from left to right, not right to left. All was well and good until my first lesson. While I'm using my bow left handed, the rest of the musicians are going with their right hand thus creating a "cross bow" effect. Dr. Phillips, the music teacher with his halo of hair would look at me and say "Anita, the violin is not for you". Not to be discouraged, I played for my own enjoyment and to the laughter of my sisters.

I graduated in 1944 from Beverly High School, was voted the best dancer with Ross Roberts and that was because we danced in a play we were in. I had the acting bug starting in my Junior year and also acted in the Senior play. Do I still think I'm a "nobody?" I'm working on being some one to be proud of, it doesn't happen overnight. While going to school, I had a job working Saturdays at W. T. Grants during Christmas and also worked at Almy's Department store. Would you believe they put me in the "undergarments" department where I had to go into the fitting room to measure ladies for "foundations". Oh what a time when I had to literally throw the measure tape around her to find her size. After that episode, Norma, my friend was also working at Almy's, we'd get behind the counter, scoot down and laugh at what we had to do. Most of our male classmates were in the service and as we wanted to do our part for the war our school donated our time to rolling bandages, Safety Patrol, Minute Men Volunteers, Salvage group, selling War Bonds, Letter writing to the troops to name a few.

When graduation came around, my brother brought home a sailor for me to go to the dance. We were four couples getting together to go to Chickland after the dance, but as gas was rationed, we all had our parents siphon enough gas to get us to and from Chickland. Thank heavens none of our parent smoked, siphoning gas is bad enough, but, well, you get the picture.

Also at this time, at the age of 18, I started dating a Marine, John McCarthy from the next town, Salem.. He also received my scroll letters. My first heartbreak. He came home but didn't call me. My best friend Norma had seen him and told me he was home. How could that be? We wrote of our deep love for each other. Now, remember, this is 1944; good girls did not call on boys. What is a heartbroken girl to do? I'll tell you, I called his home, his mother answered and when I asked to speak with John, she told me he was going to become a priest and I was not to bother him. Do you remember your first heart break? I couldn't eat, cried, and my sister Rita told me it would get better. She recommended I go to modeling school to get over my first love. OK, that was a good idea. I took the train from Beverly to Boston one night a week and learned how to walk, I know, this is a different kind of walk with a book on your head. Did you ever hear of walking around with a book on your head?

Anita (front row second to the left)

Let me tell you, it helps with your posture, so much for books. I met about a dozen girls, some prettier than others but, I ranked right up there with them. I was 5' 1", 102 pounds, dark brown curly hair, dark eyes and a sense of humor. That helps when things seem to much to bear, laugh it off and that's what I did.

Somehow I got through that year. I would take the train to the USO in Boston and dance with the servicemen. I guess that was the beginning of my patriotic feelings. Remember, this is 1944, it was safe. I would dance till 11:30, take the train home, and write in my diary of the wonderful feeling I had, helping the war effort. I also took the bus to Salem Willows and danced with the Coast Guard guys stationed there.

OK, I'm going to jump back a bit to tell you of my next love. He was a year ahead of me, in high school and we would make eyes at each other. Then he joined the Navy and the next thing I knew, I was in love again. Bill Morris was his name. We dated before he was sent overseas. Before he left, silly boy, told me to date, not to sit at home waiting for his return. August of 1945 the war ended! What a happy time. My sisters, Rita and Glory and I took the bus to Salem and joined the crowd of well wishes, hugging and kissing everyone. Memories.

During this time I had a job at Sylvania Electric in Salem as an order expeditor, answering letters and letting them know when to expect delivery. In high school, I had taken Gregg Shorthand, didn't do too bad but, during the summer when vacations are taken, Mr. Lauren White came out to the group of workers and asked if anyone took shorthand. As no one raised their hand, I half raised mine and the next thing I knew I was taking dictation. I was cool with the Dear Sir; this is in answer to your letter of (date) requesting when to expect your, (OK this is new stuff) order of "incandescent, and fluorescent lighting". I'm still with in-can-des-cent shorthand when he is almost to the end of his letter with "yours truly". I took 11 pages of shorthand and swore never to volunteer again.

My next place of employment was in Beverly, the United Shoe Machinery Corp. where I worked in payroll. This was fun, each Tuesday, four of us from payroll, would go to the First National Bank, be locked in the safe area and make the payrolls in cash for over 100 workers. (I'm guessing at the number of workers, it could be more.)

Every envelope was double checked to the number of coins, dollars and then put in the envelopes, then locked in the bank until Friday payday when the armored truck would deliver it to be passed out to the workers. (I left this job to move with my parents to California)

OK, ready for my next love? Love works in mysterious ways as you are about to learn. Remember Norma, my best friend? Well, we are now 20 years old, 1946, the men are starting to return home. Remember the song: Where the Boys Are", we knew where they were so dressed to the 9's, we went to Beverly Farms, to the Tunnapoo Inn for dinner and look around. Whew, have you heard of love at first sight? Yea, I know I've told you of my young love but this was the real thing! I looked across the room at two hunks stacking shot glasses into a pyramid and my eyes latched onto this tall, handsome guy. We didn't meet but he had won my heart, little did he know, he would become my husband one year later. I said to Norma, see that guy over there? I'm going to marry him. He didn't have a chance. I didn't even know his name.

Anita and Bill (1946)

The year was 1946 and my mother needed an operation and I would take the bus to visit her at the hospital... Can you guess what was to happen? The bus driver was "thee" one, my true love. I sat at the rear of the bus and he tilted his mirror to look at me. I thought I'd end up in the next bed to my mother with my heart going pitter-patter. I got off the bus, visited my mother and back on the bus for the return trip home. I managed to be the the last to get off the bus, he held out his hand and, are you ready for this? He asked me for a date! This was November 2nd, 1946 remember this date. The very next night we had our first date. He came to my home on Mulberry Street. He didn't have a car as he was waiting for his military pay, but love overlooked all that. We held hands and walked over the Beverly-Salem bridge to the restaurant at Howard Johnsons. My stomach had butterflies; I hardly tasted my meal and was looking forward to the walk home. November in Massachusetts can be very cold, but it didn't matter, I had my love to keep me warm.

We sat on my front steps and kissed and he said, "will you marry me?" Am I dreaming? I said yes! But then he had to spoil it by saying let's go to the bus barn and make love! I said "if you love me, you will marry me, didn't you say that? "Well that poured cold water over that love affair. Remember the other guy stacking shot glasses?

Well, his name was Bill Scotti and oh, did I forget to tell you my "true loves" name was also Bill, Dwyer that is. I didn't hear from him as the "Bill's" went to Florida for a visit and when he came back, still didn't get in touch. My heart was really broken. But Norma came to the rescue again. She worked for the telephone company and as they were having a Cotillion dance, she asked me if I wanted to go. I hadn't been dating but she said, did I know Bill Dwyer was back in town? She saw him working at Silver Electric in Salem. Again, good girls did not pursue guys, but, what is a girl to do when the answer to her prayers have popped up again. Boldly I took the bus to Salem, went to Silver Electric, my heart stopped, there he was, my true love. I went up to the counter and bold as brass, asked if he would like to take me to the Cotillion. I won't keep you in suspense, he said "yes, he'd loved to take me to the dance". That was the beginning of a true love romance. We dated, held hands and yes kissed, but that was as far as it went.

OK, there has to be a downside to this story and here it is. I am now 6 months shy of my 21st birthday and still living at home. Where my parents go, so does the "live in daughter."

My parents not only owned the home we lived in, but a 3 apartment building and a beautiful gingerbread trimmed home they had been selling. Sure I knew they were selling off their property, but I didn't know they were planning on moving to California. Needless to say I went with them. Bill and I kept in touch, phone calls and air-mail, blue onion-skin letters went back and forth across the country. I still have all those mushy worded letters tied with ribbon.

Going across country with my mother and father was scary. We had a new Hudson, blue with those side wings as part of the window. I think my father enjoyed the trip of sight seeing more than I or my mother. Pops would say, "oh look at Niagra Falls" and the car would veer in that direction and my mother would grab the metal strip on the side wing of the window. This went with every sight, Grand Canyon, Old Faithful, all this was over narrow roads hugging the side of deep cliffs. My Pop got us to California without a mishap or a ticket.

Surprise, on my 21st birthday, September 14th, Bill sent me an engagement ring and asked me to marry him. I'm in heaven; all my wishes have come true. My oldest sister, Helen and her husband Fred asked if I would like to come back home and stay with them until the wedding. That is what I did, one month before our wedding. Remember the first date I had with Bill? Remember it was November 2, 1946? Well, we married on that date, November 2, 1947. I wore white, need I say more? We spent our first night at the Statler Hotel in Boston and then on to Washington, D. C. We went to all the historical places and then to a movie to see "Forever Amber". Remember this movie? It was ahead of its time, racy was the word.

We lived in Beverly for 5 months; Bill worked in Bill Scotti's Furniture store until his G.I. payment came through. Those were wonderful months of marriage, poor as the proverbial church mouse but oh, so happy.

Our first Thanksgiving was 3 weeks after our marriage. This could be a story in its self. I failed to mention, growing up, my mother did everything. I didn't even know how to boil water. What a big surprise I was in for. Back in the "old days", stoves did not have automatic igniters for the oven. As is true today, there is the Big Thanksgiving Game that Bill wanted to go see. I asked before you go, please light the oven so I can cook the chicken. With a kiss and a hug, the pilot light was lit and off to the football game he goes, leaving me to cook my very first meal, let alone Thanksgiving dinner.

This could be another story in its self also. I was learning as I went along. I did know to take the parts out of the cavity of the chicken before cooking. And I did know how to boil potatoes, having watched Mama. I also knew enough to buy peas, an angel food cake, whipped cream for the meal. But what is a holiday without an apple pie? Don't laugh yet, the best is yet to come.

I played with the flour, eggs mixture like it was play dough which I'm familiar with, spread it over pie tin, sliced apples to the level of the pie tin, but wait, I don't have any ground cinnamon, but I did have cinnamon sticks, so, I broke these up and scattered them through the apples and covered with more" play" dough. I was quite proud of this feat. I had put the chicken in the oven, started boiling the peas and potatoes, set the table and waited for Bill to come home to our first Thanksgiving meal. Hugs and kisses, then I open the oven door and lo and behold, the chicken is as naked as when I had put it in. I didn't know I was supposed to turn the heat up. The potatoes and peas were done, so, we sat and ate them. Bill turned the heat up for the oven to cook the chicken to eat later. When the pie was completely cooked, I proudly took it out of the oven and served my new husband a piece of hot pie. When he dug in, he asked what cigar butts were doing in the pie! I explained it was cinnamon sticks and cried. I got rewarded with a hug and kiss. We did enjoy the cake and whipped cream. My mother didn't have any faith in my cooking, not even to make a cup of tea, the water was never hot enough, potatoes either had too much or not enough salt. I have to admit, today I am a great cook and love to cook for crowds.

I'd like to take you back to 1946, as you know, the war had ended, and the Fourth of July was a big celebration, with the USS Missouri battleship anchored off the next town, Marblehead. My brother Maxwell, an Ensign in the navy got special treatment when we went out on the duck to tour the ship. OK, a little personal history. I am 20 years old, single, want to impress the sailors. I'm dressed in a teal wrap-around top, white skirt, spectator pumps, long curly hair, red lipstick. On the way to the ship, a shower hit us in the duck and the rain stopped just as we arrived to board the ship. The sailors are squatted down along the inner deck waiting to go ashore. Remember I said I wanted to impress the sailors? Well, after touring an upper deck, we started down the steps and being very lady like, I decided I could step from the second (not the first step) to the deck. I forgot the deck was slick with the rain, so, drum roll, from the second step to the, wait a minute, to the skidding across the deck on my white skirt, past the waiting sailors, was my exit. I should have been embarrassed but not as much as my brother. Ah memories. Did you know I slid to the spot the peace treaty between Japan and the United States was signed years later? It is now roped off with a round plaque immortalizing that final day.

It is now April, 1948, Bill had received his G.I. money and we decided to move to California to start our new life. We didn't have much, mostly clothes and some boxed wedding presents. I was looking forward to moving to warm sunshine and not have to wear heavy clothing, including a beautiful lynx jacket. Before we moved, I sold all my winter wear and yes, including my lynx jacket. Little did I know, California has cold spells. I could have brought my lynx jacket. OK, side note; there was no PETA back then.

California here we come. We took the Greyhound bus across the country, to Santa Barbara, California where my parents lived. When we arrived at the bus station, after traveling 4 days, day and night, I went to the rest room to freshen up before meeting my parents as a married woman with a new husband. I brushed my teeth and threw up. No big deal, blame it on the food we ate at the rest stops. ugh.

My mother was not fond of Bill as he had broken my heart and she was afraid he would do it again, but she did welcome us. My parents picked us up and took us to their home. on Gravilla Drive. It was a happy reunion, all talking at the same time. Remember I am 21, lived a very sheltered life so when I threw up 2 more days in a row, I mentioned it to my mother and she asked "could you be pregnant?" Huh? Me? O.K., you're thinking I should know about the birds and the bees, sure but, was I pregnant?? I sure found out in a hurry when Bill, who was a smoker, kissed me and I "woofed my cookies", not just one day, but for days each morning until I told him not to kiss me. This is the beginning of what I didn't know, trust me, no one would make this up, especially about themselves.

We moved from my parent's house to what used to be an old army barracks called Hoff Heights where a lot of policemen and families lived. It was a friendly time. OK, we're in a new state, unfamiliar with Santa Barbara but Bill is trying to find a job. Have you ever heard of pots called Kitchen Craft? That is what Bill sold, setting up home parties, it was hard but he did well. Great, we had money coming in so we rented a downstairs apartment from the Swaffords, a nice elderly couple on Cota St. Bill's next job was as a long haul driver for

Bekins Van and Storage and traveled for days at a time, leaving me home alone.

We had made new friends, Bob, Carmen, Barbara, Myron, Marie and Phil to name a few. We did a lot of things together. It was fun as Carmen and I were both pregnant, due about the same time. We'd go to Ojai, Wheeler Springs, eat the best chili, the guys drank beer, we'd wade in the springs. We would go to each other's home and play Canasta but when Peyton Place came on the TV, the game stopped and all eyes turned to the TV. I remember one time the guys were playing poker and us girls would chat and knit. I decided I wanted to learn to play poker, and because I was pregnant, they put up with me. They dealt 7 cards and the bidding started. I held my cards close to my belly and bid along with the guys. I won! When they asked me what I had, I proudly said "three pairs". It pays to be pregnant sometimes. Memorable times.

I gained over 30 pounds and my stomach, when I sat, extended to the end of my knees. My inverted belly button became an "outie" and I worried about the baby. When I went to Dr. Patterson I told him I was worried the baby (I'm not making this up!) would pop through my belly button, could he please tape my belly??? Well, you know, the umbilical cord, when you're born, ties you to your mother. I now call it the" imbecilical cord".

Because of being so naive, was I in for a rude awakening when it was time to deliver. I was 2 weeks overdue so - - -they gave me castor oil and did it ever work!! I was in delivery and after 12 hours of labor, how appropriately named, my 8 ½ pound son was born, December 18, 1948. I'll save you the time of counting the months from when I married to the delivery date. I got pregnant after the wedding. Bill arrived after the birth and was overjoyed to see a bouncing baby boy we named William Joseph Dwyer after Bill and my father.

Duh, there may be books on bringing up a baby but how could they? Each baby is a new individual, cries, sleeps, eats and yes poops. I felt like I was playing dolls with my baby until one day he cried and cried so hard, the soft scalp was separating. I was in a panic, Bill was on the road, what to do. I called our landlord, Mrs. Swafford and she came down and told me not to worry, this happens as their heads have not grown together yet. Whew. Billy was a great baby, he liked to sleep and I'd wake to feed him, tuck him back into his crib. My parents spoiled him; baby sat him, visited all the time. Bill and I were a family.

Bill

Bill was now working for the Santa Barbara Police Department, different shifts but when he worked the four to midnight shift, he would come home, put Billy on his lap and drive up State Street when the Christmas trees were lite. This would help getting Billy to sleep the whole night.

Carmen also had a baby boy, Craig and we compared their growth, first word, first steps and bragged about our boys. When the boys were 18 months old, Santa Barbara Fiesta was a special time in Santa Barbara. We made blue taffeta toreador outfits with sequins for them to wear.

My father made a replica of the Santa Barbara Old Mission and we entered them into the parade. We were so proud when they received a ribbon.

As young mothers, Carm and I would compare their accomplishments and decided when we would have another baby. I said, I wanted a baby girl with golden curls, blue eyes and not for another three and half years. Surprise! Billy was born on December 18, 1948 and Donna Suzann Dwyer was born on June 18, 1952, exactly three and a half years later. All you have to do is wish and it comes true.

When it comes to babies, no two are alike. Billy would sleep, Donna would cry when Bill and I would go out, she'd throw her baby bottle across the room. We had a great babysitter, Mrs. Ellis, lived next door and only charged us 35 cents an hour. Before Bill and I would go out for the evening, I would get dressed then wrap my bathrobe over my dress, go say "nite nite". She would be happy, thinking we were in for the night. I could go on but you get the picture. Even if I have to say it myself, she was adorable. She had curly reddish blond curly hair and blue eyes. My wish had come true. With two babies, I stayed home and Bill worked. He not only worked on the Police Force, but detailed cars and bartended at the Miramar Hotel in Montecito He was a great provider and I truly loved being a mom. One thing I did I regret now, is make my children clean their plates. Donna would sit and pout and say "NO", her favorite word.

With 2 children and only 2 bedrooms, it was time to look for a home to buy. With Bill's 6 years and 6 days serving in the Army, we were able to buy our first home with a GI loan. A cute 2 bedroom, large corner lot on Calle Laureles. Yes, I know, we still had only 2 bedrooms but it was a step up from Hoff Heights. The price will surprise you. We borrowed $200 from my parents for the down payment of this

$8,950 home. Another policeman and his wife, John and Darlene lived two houses from us and we became friends.

Darlene's uncle owned the Blue Onion on upper State St., a drive- in with car hops. On a dare, Darlene asked if I would car hop with her. ha. Little did I know what I was getting into. At least it wasn't on roller skates.

We trained on how to hook the tray on the door window and the menu items. " Our" first day of work, Darlene didn't show up but as I was there, why not work! We kept the menus in pouches on our side. OK, I'm ready for the first car, go up to the car window and asked what can I get you. Cool? huh. They ordered hamburger, fries and buttermilk. I placed the order, walked up to the car and as I was placing the tray on the window, the buttermilk tipped and spilled into my menu pouch! Do you know what that smells like? I finished the day and gave notice.

You may think Darlene was a bad influence on me when you read the following. She had 5 children, I had 2 and Elaine had 3. We were all living paycheck to paycheck and couldn't afford to buy magazines -so-, we found out when the vender changed the stores magazine racks and we would pile the ten kids in two cars and off we'd go to the city dump. Before he could empty his truck of unsold magazines, we'd be right on him, pick up comic books, Ladies Home Journal, Police Crime Stoppers (for our husbands,) and movie magazines. We'd fill our boxes and felt like Santa Claus. We all were happy with our finds. How's that for a memory? You learn to make do. From Calle Laureles, we moved to San Pablo Ln, 3 bedrooms with a detached garage. The driveway was so narrow, you almost scraped your elbow on the fence. This house was $16,500 and we did it all by ourselves, no borrowing from my parents. Did I mention I didn't know how to drive? After Billy was born and about 18 months old, Bill would give me driving lessons in our green, 4 door Buick, I think it was a 1934 model. We'd put Billy in the back seat removable carriage seat and I would get behind the wheel and Bill would direct me what to do. I would get a nervous stomach each time I would drive. I'm proud to say, in my sixty plus years of driving I only got one ticket and I deserved it for speeding.

Bill is still with the police department and on rainy days, he would come home in the police car and take all the kids from the neighborhood to school. This would be frowned upon now but back then, it taught them to respect policemen. They learned they were parents also.

It is now 1958 and both Billy and Donna (I call her Doedi, but don't you even think about it) were in school so I decided to get a part time job so I would be home when they came home from school. I applied at the Santa Barbara News Press and got a part time job working for Bert Willowby in accounting. It worked perfectly, I was paid, and I was home and I was becoming a somebody.

We now had money in the bank, not much but not only were we happy, we had plans to buy a four bedroom home. So - - - we shopped around and John Cox was building two story homes on Patterson Ave. This was 1964 and it wasn't a great time to be selling or buying homes. We looked at the models and liked the downstairs of one model and the upstairs of another model. After "haggling" price, lot size and wanting the upstairs of one and the downstairs of the other, John Cox agreed to our purchase. The price was $24,500. Interest rates were 18%! We took pictures of the progress of the building of our dream home.

As the difference of the two homes was slightly off, we got an extra foot added on the back of the home. About this time, luck was to strike again. Friends of ours, had the liquor concession at the Santa Barbara Polo Club and they asked if we would be interested in the part-time job. After talking this over, we decided how could we go wrong. The answer was YES. This is still 1964, Bill is still with the police department and we found between the two of us, we could operate the bar at the Polo Club. I would open the bar on the days they played polo and Bill would come after work. These were truly the best years of our lives. When Bob Skene, a 10 goal player and manager of the club asked me if I could type, I answered yes! From then on, I not only typed, I billed the polo players, made arrangements for hotel rooms, when there was a party, I would help with arrangements. I was even chosen Queen of the Polo Club, how about that!

Anita (Queen of the Polo Club) and husband Bill

The biggest feat was in 1968-69, they were planning a Polo Ball at the Coral Casino and I was in charge of seating arrangements. The round tables seated 8 or 4 couples. When it came to the single seating arrangements, no problem I thought. Little did I know the single gentleman and the single lady were divorced from each other but they were good sports. The highlight of the evening was the guest. The Shah of Iran was in attendance.

Anita (standing at the middle)

Others in attendance were Jane Mansfield and Mickey Hargitay and Bill and I were seated at their table, not of my making. The players were very nice to us, they invited us to their homes and parties.

Have you ever sat astride a Clydesdale? One of the polo players had invited Bill and I up to their home in northern California. Lo and behold, and I mean behold! They sat me on a beautiful Clydesdale horse, my legs extended right and left! Know what? I wasn't afraid, they are such gentle horses. Again, memories. This all ended in 1969 when the owner of the club, Mr. Ruddy Tongg sold the fields and they were closed for a season. I truly missed this job, I use the word "job" loosely, and it was my second heaven.

Life was a gift and Bill and I and our children treasured every minute. As both Bill and I depended on the income from the liquor concession, I started to look for a job. Bill was bartending at the Miramar but that was not enough income. Luck would have it again. My friend Susie worked at a law firm in Santa Barbara and told me of a receptionist job opening. I went for the interview and got the job. Not only was I receptionist, but relief switchboard operator. Later they made me in charge of support personnel. There were 17 attorneys and as many support workers. I loved this job and when we moved to Lompoc, I got a rave recommendation. Somewhere along the way, my parents divorced, my mother moved to Florida and my Pops stayed in Santa Barbara. His hobby was carving and he would take all of his beautiful carvings to Cabrillo Blvd each Sunday to display them. He has had his work displayed at the Smithsonian in Washington, D.C, at the Santa Barbara Old Mission, The Space Center, gifts to Congressman Lagomarsino and Secretary of State, March Fong Eu, Lawrence Welk and others. He loved his country, the United States of America.

My mother would visit, knowing Monday nights Pops would come for dinner. They didn't speak to each other. The tension could be felt but what was one to do? In 1969 when my mother was visiting, the kids were in our pool, oh, did I forget to mention this? Yes, we had a pool with a slide and practically lived in it. Anyway, there was a loud noise, I asked the kids, is everything all right and they said the noise came from upstairs. Oh my God, when I got to Bill in the bathroom, there was blood coming from his nose and mouth. I called Dr. Flynn, our family Dr., told him of Bill bleeding and he sent an ambulance and met us at St. Francis Hospital. He had a bleeding ulcer and as fast as they fed blood, he rejected it. For every pint of blood he received, we had to replace it doubly. As he was still a policeman, the prisoners donated blood in his name. A total of 36 pints. They performed last rights on him and I leaned over him and said "don't you dare die, I don't have a decent black dress for your funeral". You see, we did a lot of going out nights and dressing up, me in mostly black cocktail dresses so you see, they were not fit for his funeral. Would you believe he survived? It was slow but he was with us. Thank you God. In 1980, we sold our home on Patterson Ave and made a tidy profit and moved to Lompoc, California, 50 miles up the coast.

In 1980 we bought a cocktail lounge and oh how we worked. Bill bartended, managed it and I did the books. We made a success of DJ'S, kept the doors open from 10 am to 2 am. The couple that had owned it before us, Duke and Elaine, asked if he could come back and be a partner. After some negotiations, Duke became a 30% owner. We had DJ'S until 1997 and had to sell it as Bill was not able to carry out his duties. We had a great time and still have many friends we met along the way.

Here is another story.

Our son is married and he and his wife Victoria lived in Chula Vista and our daughter, and George lived in Ventura at this time. We planned to meet at our home in Lompoc. As we couldn't get together for Christmas, we planned to all meet in February, 1995. It started out a fun day, throwing firewood over the back fence, laughing, when all of sudden Bill fell, and Billy and Vicki immediately started CPR on him yelling for me to call 911. He had had a heart attack!

Somehow, the neighbors heard the commotion and formed a circle and prayed. The ambulance came and took him to Lompoc Hospital emergency room. As luck would have it, Dr. Coughlin, the best heart Dr. around, was just leaving the hospital and they had him quickly work on Bill. He told me not to expect miracles as his heart was not beating, but thank you God, his heart started. He was in a coma and I leaned over his bed and said "Don't you dare die, I don't have a decent black dress". Know what? He must have heard me and was transferred to a rehab center in Santa Barbara where he remained for three weeks.

One day I got permission to take him for a ride and asked where he would like to go. He said home to take a shower and shampoo. I piled him in the car and as I was driving past Patterson Ave., he said he wanted to go home. I told him we had moved to Lompoc and there was where I was taking him. And take him I did, 50 miles up and 50 miles back and he did get his shower and shampoo.

When he was finally discharged and I got him home, he was so sweet. I taught him to read, tell time, and ask questions. When asked who was President, he said "Nixon". In 1995? I started him reading Dr. Susess and painted the clock on the 12. 3, 6, 9 with red nail polish. His writing was better than before his attack. See there is always a bright side, only if you look.

I would take him out for rides and lunch to Buellton, Pismo Beach and Santa Barbara. His taste buds were gone but when he got to Split Pea Anderson's and had a bowl of split pea, his eyes lit up and he said he could taste! We continued to make progress. Our Daughter and George were finally going to tie the knot and marry in May. You know how plans have a way of changing. Bill was looking forward to walking Donna down the aisle and put on his best beige suit but this was not to be.

January 27, 2001 he had another heart attack and this time, did not come back, even with my black dress not suitable. Again the ambulance came and took him to the hospital where he was pronounced dead. I told the Dr. on duty, he did this before, he will come back but he said no, handed me his stethoscope to listen, his heart is not beating. You never are prepared, even with the 2 "dress" rehearsals, you are not ready to accept it. Donna and George married March 24, 2001 without her dad to walk her down the aisle. Her brother, Billy did the honors. We put Bill's ashes by the alter so he would be in attendance. Memories can be good even when there is sadness. You learn to deal with it. After 53 of marriage I find I'm now a widow. I was sad, lonely but I did have his ashes and talked with him and hoped he heard me. After his death, about 4 years later, I tore down the wall I had built around me and wrote a self published book, "Life, Love, Loss, the Empty Chair" It was catharsis baring my soul. There was a Vietnam Vet living in Lompoc who had been infected with Agent Orange. He made his living as a singer but because of his health, had to give up singing. ` The residence of Lompoc had fund raisers for him and I donated $5. from each book sale I made. For self selling, I did good. I donated $875 to his cause. Some good deed comes from sadness.

I started dating, met some local men but none was "the one". I've been called a "senior cougar" at age 84, as not only did I go on line and start dating, but I met a man 11 year younger than I, but and this is a great "but," we met at a local restaurant on August 18, 2011. As he walked through the door, I said to myself," he is a keeper."

Carl, my love

We hit it off, like two peas in a pod; we'd finish or say the same thing at the same time. He "cheated," he looked me up in the local newspaper. He was impressed with what he had read. We have kept our own places and continue dating and have "sleep over's". Not one to blow my own horn, but I now think I'm a" somebody", but it doesn't make me feel any different. My accomplishments are: After I retired: I helped 1st graders at the local schools, received a Golden Apple award, was an Ambassador with the Lompoc Chamber of Commerce, chaired 2 of the 12 years, produced and published a calendar for the Chamber of Commerce titled "Masked Mystery Maidens", using local business women as models, have written over 70 poems, self published. Received a trophy from World of Poetry for "Our Flag," self published "Life, Love, Loss, the Empty Chair" and for the best to come, published "George the Giraffe" (now on Amazon) and now at the young age of 88 writing "Kenny the Kangaroo & Koala" telling of their escapades.

Mayor Dick De Wees and Anita (WOTM 2005)

In 2005 chosen Woman of the Year Lompoc, won the "bed" trophy as the best theme, as Mae West and oh yes, self published "How Did We Get Into This Mell of a Hess". At age 83, I acted in 9 live performances of "Over the River Through the Woods, at Lompoc Civic Theater.

And now, a drum roll please, I finished 8 weeks of drum lessons. Yes, at 88 year young.

The brain is a wonderful thing, it has so much stored and we only touch the surface. Remember I mentioned learning from Bill Clinton.? I saw a movie with Catherine Deneuve where she would talk on the phone with men, breathing heavily, and saying oh yes!, well naive me, I thought that was "oral sex". It took a president to educate me! Let me pause and check my brain to see if I've left any thing out or that I'm willing to share.

I've been asked what is the "secret" to my "get up and go". I can touch my toes, walk fast so that death can not catch me and enjoy each day as if it were my last. I also have a saying, "I'll go to your funeral if you will come to mine". Impossible. Remember my meeting "a keeper"? His name is Carl. We will be celebrating our four year anniversary in

August. We have too much fun, we love going to jazz festivals, taking cruises, sharing laughter, holding hands and yes, kissing. Remember, you too can have fun after 50 or older and the loss of your mate. Life is for the living.

Winning the bed race

Bill and Vicky

Donna and George

My "children", now in their 60's make my life complete, we can talk on the same level, understand what life has dealt us and know they didn't come through my belly button. There is no ending to this story. I now consider that I've become a "Somebody" but I don't feel any different, only wiser. To A Continued Life, Love.

Thank you and I hope you enjoyed this story.

Anita Dwyer

"TO WHO WHO"

It was a happy day, family gathered around
Suddenly he toppled, like a tree, he fell to ground
His heart had stopped, was it never to start beating
　　　　　Again?
His son and daughter in- law quickly worked with
　　　　　CPR, but still he would not bend
9-1-1, the medics, doctors and nurses all worked
　　　　　To make him live
They paddled, needled, pounded, yet his heart
　　　　　Would not give
The hearts of many felt the pain and prayed, his
　　　　　Life be spared
From up above, He answered the call and showed
　　　　　He really cared
His life came slowly back, his heart started to
　　　　　Beat and flutter
The joy was shared, tears were shed, no words
　　　　　Could we utter
The heart and mind are a wonder of working with
　　　　　One another
Slowly the progress, but what pleasure to hear
　　　　　His voice, his laughter

I love you "Who Who"

2001

About the author

She was born in Beverly, Massachusetts in 1926, the youngest of 5 children. As this was during the Great Depression, money was scarce, you learn to live with it. Graduated in 1944, during the Second World War and straight from high school to work.

In her book she tells of these jobs, if jobs can be called funny, she makes it so. If life during the 40's can be memorable, she has done a great job to entertain you. Loves were few but each was full of meaning.

Her children are her pride and joy and both are retired

You are never too old to seek new love (on the internet), she is now called a "Senior Cougar" by her friends. She lives life to be enjoyed and shared it with her second love she met in the internet.

Printed in the United States
By Bookmasters